More Than a Dozen
HATS & BEANIES™

Carri Hammett

Annie's®

A Note From the Designer

. . . .

Making hats is one of the best ways for a knitter to explore creativity and learn new techniques. Knitted hats are also quick to make and a great project to use when you want to experiment with yarn and color without making a big investment. In this book, you'll find a diverse collection of hats and beanies for both adults and children. The various patterns are written for a wide range of skills, so knitters of every level will enjoy using this book, and those who are new to knitting hats and beanies will love the basic tutorial. With careful attention to the design details, you'll find patterns that are easy to use and fun to make!

Carri Hammett

Contents

Chunky Lace Beanie,
page 18

Color Brick Stitch,
page 16

Hugs & Kisses,
page 38

Basic Hat Tutorial

To make a simple hat you will need a 16-inch circular needle, a set of double-point needles in the same size, a round stitch marker and a blunt tapestry needle.

Using the circular needle, cast on the number of stitches called for in the pattern. The most important part of joining the stitches in the round is a warning you will see in most hat patterns that you should be "careful not to twist the stitches." The chain of cast-on stitches must not spiral around the needle. In order to avoid this problem, always make sure the bumps at the bottom of the cast-on stitches are lined up facing the center of the circle formed by the needle as shown below.

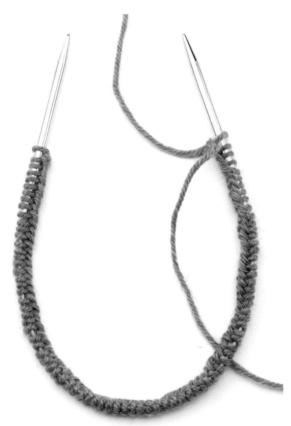

After checking that the stitches are properly aligned, hold the needle tips so the first stitch that was cast on (the slip knot) is on the left-hand tip and the last stitch (connected to the working yarn) is on the right-hand tip. Before working the first stitch of the first round, put a stitch marker on the right-hand tip.

As shown in the photo above, insert the right-hand tip into the first stitch on the left-hand tip and use the working yarn to make a stitch, thereby joining the stitches and making a circle. On this first stitch, pull the yarn firmly to avoid a gap. Continue knitting around until you reach the stitch marker which indicates that you have completed one round. Slip the marker from the left-hand tip to right-hand tip and continue knitting. The marker is known as the beginning-of-round marker and each time you knit to it, one round has been completed.

Continue knitting around and around until the body of the hat (measured from the cast-on edge) is the length specified by the pattern as the point to begin shaping the crown. The crown shaping is accomplished by dividing the stitches into wedges or sections (often marked) and gradually decreasing the number of stitches per section to form a tapered top. As the stitch count decreases, the circumference of the hat becomes smaller and the stitches can no longer be stretched around the circular needle. At that point, the stitches must be transferred to double-point needles as shown below, to finish the remainder of the crown. Knit the stitches off the circular needle and onto four double-point needles. If possible, the number of stitches should be divided evenly, and the beginning-of-round marker should be in the middle of one of the needles.

Once all the stitches have been transferred, use the fifth needle to continue knitting, as illustrated in the photo below. Knit all the stitches from the first needle onto the free needle. When that needle is empty, it becomes the new free needle and is used to knit the stitches on the next needle, and so on, around the hat.

Upon reaching the final round, just a few stitches will be left, as you can see below. Cut the working yarn, leaving a tail at least 10 inches long and thread it on a blunt tapestry needle. Thread the tail through each of the stitch loops on the top of the hat in the same order that you knit them.

Pull the tail firmly to close the hole in the top of the hat. Pass the tail (still threaded on the needle) to the inside of the hat and, after giving it one final tug, weave it into the stitches on the wrong side of the hat to secure. •

T!P

HOW TO

If prefered, any of the hats in this book can also be made using a 40" circular needle using the Magic Loop method, found on page 44.

Basic Rolled Brim Hat

This simple hat is the perfect project for knitters who are just beginning their hat-making journey.

Skill Level
■■□□ EASY

Sizes
Small (medium, large) for average child (woman, man)

Instructions are given for smallest size, with larger sizes in parentheses. When only 1 number is given, it applies to all sizes.

Finished Measurements
Circumference: 18 (20, 22) inches
Height: 9¾ (10½, 11¼) inches

Materials
- Cascade 220 Superwash (worsted weight; 100% superwash wool; 220 yds/100g per ball): 1 ball straw #870
- Size 7 (4.5mm) double-point (set of 5) and 16-inch circular needles or size needed to obtain gauge
- Stitch markers, 1 in CC for beg of rnd

Gauge
20 sts and 28 rnds = 4 inches/10 cm in St st.

To save time, take time to check gauge.

Pattern Note
Change to double-point needles when necessary.

Hat

Body
With circular needle, cast on 90 (100, 110) sts. Mark beg of rnd and join, being careful not to twist sts.

Work in St st (knit all rnds) until piece measures 6¾ (7¼, 7¾) inches (unrolled) and on last rnd, dec 2 (4, 6) sts evenly around—88 (96, 104) sts.

Crown
Set-up rnd: *K9 (10, 11), k2tog, pm; rep from * around—80 (88, 96) sts.

Knit 1 rnd.

Dec rnd: *Knit to 2 sts before marker, k2tog; rep from * around—72 (80, 88) sts.

Rep Dec rnd [every other rnd] 8 (9, 10) times, removing all markers on last rnd—8 sts.

Cut yarn, leaving a tail at least 10 inches long. Thread tail through rem sts and pull tight to close hole in top of hat. Weave in tail on WS.

Weave in all other ends. Lightly steam-block. ●

Basic Striped Hat

Express yourself! A striped hat offers the opportunity to channel your creativity by making lots of hats with different combinations of colors and stripes.

· ·

Skill Level
◖■◧◻◗ EASY

Sizes
Small (medium, large) to fit average child (woman, man)

Instructions are given for smallest size, with larger sizes in parentheses. When only 1 number is given, it applies to all sizes.

Finished Measurements
Circumference: 18 (20, 22) inches
Height: 7½ (8½, 9½) inches

Materials
- Cascade 220 Superwash (worsted weight; 100% superwash wool; 220 yds/100g per ball): 1 ball autumn heather #868 (A) and sunset orange #808 (B)
- Size 5 (3.75mm) 16-inch circular needle
- Size 7 (4.5mm) 16-inch circular and double-point needles (set of 5) or size needed to obtain gauge
- Stitch markers, 1 in CC for beg of rnd

Gauge
20 sts and 28 rnds = 4 inches/10cm in St st with larger needle.

To save time, take time to check gauge.

Special Techniques

Starting New Colors
Stripes add interest and appeal to hats. The width of the stripes (number of rounds) dictates how the yarn is handled when it isn't being used. When you temporarily stop working with one color in order to add a stripe in the other color, it is not necessary to cut the old yarn if you will be working with that color again no more than 4 rounds later. Simply park the yarn at the beginning of the round (leave it hanging) until you are ready to use it again. When you finish making the stripe with the new color and start knitting again with the old color, simply pull the yarn up from where it was parked and start knitting again. This is known as "carrying the yarn up." The trick when starting the yarn again is to pull it firmly enough to close the last stitch where you left off using the color but not so tightly that you cause the knitting to pucker.

If you will be working more than 4 rounds before going back to the other color, it is best to cut that yarn when you are done with it and join a new end of the color when needed. This will leave tails that need to be woven in, but the overall look is much neater than carrying the yarn up between wide stripes. When adding or cutting yarn, be sure to leave a tail at least 8 inches long for weaving in.

Jogless Stripes
When knitting a hat in the round you are, in effect, making a spiral. This means that the last stitch of a round is one stitch higher than the first stitch of that round. This creates a jog in the stripes that some knitters find unattractive. To minimize this effect, use the "Jogless Stripes" technique, working the first and second round of every new stripe as follows:

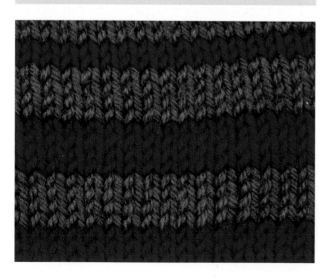

Rnd 1: Change to the new color and knit around.

Rnd 2: Slip the first stitch purlwise, then knit around.

Pattern Notes
Change to double-point needles when necessary.

If using double-point needles for the entire hat, you will need a set of 5 smaller double-point needles.

Hat

Body
Using smaller circular needle and A, cast on 88 (100, 108) sts; mark beg of rnd and join, being careful not to twist sts.

Work 7 rnds in k2, p2 rib.

Next rnd: Change to larger needle; knit and inc 2 (0, 2) sts evenly around—90 (100, 110) sts.

Knit 3 rnds.

Stripe Pattern
Note: Remember to cut the yarn or carry it up between stripes depending on number of rnds in the following stripe. If desired, use the Jogless Stripes technique.

With B, knit 8 rnds.

With A, knit 3 rnds.

With B, knit 4 rnds.

With A, knit 4 rnds.

With B, knit 2 rnds.

Sizes Medium (Large) Only
Rep [last 6 rnds] once (twice) more.

All Sizes
With A, work even until piece measures approx 4½ (5¼, 6) inches, and on last rnd, dec 2 (4, 6) sts evenly around—88 (96, 104) sts.

Crown
Set-up rnd: *K9 (10, 11), k2tog, pm; rep from * around—80 (88, 96) sts.

Knit 1 rnd.

Dec rnd: *Knit to 2 sts before marker, k2tog; rep from * around—72 (80, 88) sts.

Rep Dec rnd [every other rnd] 8 (9, 10) times, removing all markers on last rnd—8 sts.

Cut yarn, leaving a tail at least 10 inches long. Thread tail through rem sts and pull tight to close hole in top of hat. Weave in tail on WS.

Weave in all ends. Lightly steam-block. ●

Colorful Earflap Hat

Color, texture, and bold design are all included in this hat.
This hat is both fun to make and fun to give and wear.

Skill Level

■■■□ INTERMEDIATE

Sizes

Small (medium, large) for average child
(woman, man)

Instructions are given for smallest size, with
larger sizes in parentheses. When only 1 number
is given, it applies to all sizes.

Finished Measurements

Circumference: 17¾ (20, 22¼) inches
Height: 7¼ (8¼, 9¼) inches
(not including earflaps)

Materials

- Dream in Color Classy (worsted
  weight; 100% merino wool;
  250 yds/113g per hank): 1 hank each
  Bermuda teal (A), gold experience (B),
  shiny moss (C) and cinnamon girl (D)
- Size 6 (4mm) 16-inch circular and
  double-point needles (set of 3)
- Size 8 (5mm) 16-inch circular and
  double-point needles (set of 5) or size
  needed to obtain gauge
- Size H/8 (5mm) crochet hook
- Stitch markers, 1 in CC for beg of rnd

4 MEDIUM

Gauge

18 sts and 24 rnds = 4 inches/10cm in St st with
larger needle.

To save time, take time to check gauge.

Pattern Notes

Change to double-point needles when necessary.

If using double-point needles for the entire hat, you
will need a set of 5 smaller double-point needles.

Earflaps
Make 2

With smaller dpns and A, cast on 8 sts.

Rows 1 and 2: Knit.

Row 3: K1, kfb, knit to last 3 sts, kfb, k2—10 sts.

Rows 4–6: Knit.

Rep [Rows 3–6] 5 (6, 7) times—20 (22, 24) sts.

Work even in garter st until piece measures
3 (3¼, 3½) inches.

Cut yarn and set aside on spare dpn.

Hat
Begin by casting on 3 separate sets of sts as follows:

With smaller circular needle and A, cast on 7 (8, 9)
sts, cut yarn; leaving the first set of sts in place, cast
on 26 (30, 34) sts, cut yarn; cast on 7 (8, 9) sts, do not
cut yarn, turn.

Set-up rnd: K7 (8, 9), knit across first earflap, k26
(30, 34), knit across second earflap, k7 (8, 9); mark
beg of rnd and join, being careful not to twist sts—
80 (90, 100) sts.

Purl 1 rnd.

Continuing in garter st (knit 1 rnd, purl 1 rnd),
*work 2 more rnds with A, 2 rnds with B, 2 rnds
with C; rep from * once more.

Change to larger needle and A; **knit 3 (4, 5) rnds.

With D, knit 1 rnd and purl 1 rnd.

With A, knit 2 rnds.

With B, knit 2 rnds.

Next rnd: With C, *k1, sl 1; rep from * around.

Next rnd: With C, *p1, sl 1; rep from * around.

With A, knit 2 rnds.

With D, knit 1 rnd, purl 1 rnd.

Rep from ** once more.

With A, work even in St st (knit all rnds) until piece measures 5 (5¾, 6½) inches from cast-on edge (not counting earflaps) and on last rnd, dec 0 (2, 4) sts evenly around—80 (88, 96) sts.

Crown
Set-up rnd: *K8 (9, 10), k2tog, pm; rep from * around—72 (80, 88) sts.

Knit 1 rnd.

T!P

HOW TO

It is not necessary to cut yarn A when other colors are being used. Let the yarn hang loose when not in use. When knitting the next stripe with yarn A, be sure the first stitch isn't pulled too tightly. The other colors should be cut when not in use and the ends woven in.

Dec rnd: Knit to 2 sts before marker, k2tog; rep from * around—64 (72, 80) sts.

Continue in St st and rep Dec rnd [every other rnd] 7 (8, 9) times, removing markers on last rnd—8 sts.

Cut yarn, leaving a tail at least 10 inches long. Thread tail through rem sts and pull tight to close hole in top of hat. Weave in tail on WS.

Finishing
Weave in all other ends. Block.

Edging
With smaller needle and D and beg at center back with RS facing, pick up and knit approx 104 (118, 132) sts around the hat bottom and earflap edges, picking up 1 st in each cast-on st and 3 sts for every 4 rows along sides of earflaps; do not join, turn.

Knit 1 row, turn.

Loosely bind off all sts.

Cut yarn; use tail to make small seam between first and last edge sts.

Top Braids
Cut 2 (24-inch) strands each of B, C and D.

Thread yarn needle with 3 strands (1 each color); pass from one side to the other of the top hole with half the length on either side of the hole. Rep with the other 3 strands, positioning them at a 90-degree angle to the first set. Tie all strands into an overhand knot secured close to the hat.

Using all 3 colors for each braid, make 2 braids 6 inches long or to desired length. Tie an overhand knot at the end of each braid to secure; trim yarn.

Earflap Braids
Cut 2 (30-inch) strands each of B, C and D.

Use crochet hook to pull all 6 strands from RS to WS at center bottom of earflap, then pull strands to RS again. Leaving a slack loop on the WS of the flap, pull until all 12 ends are even. Reach through the loop with thumb and forefinger and pull all of the ends through the loop (like making fringe on the bottom of a scarf). Pull to snug the loop on the earflap bottom edge.

Using all 12 strands, make a braid 8 inches long or to desired length. Tie an overhand knot at the end of the braid to secure; trim yarn. ●

Aussie Hat

Add some "down under" to your knitting repertoire with this alpaca-trimmed hat (sorry sheep!).

Skill Level

■■■□ INTERMEDIATE

Sizes

Small (medium, large) to fit average child (woman, man)

Instructions are given for smallest size, with larger sizes in parentheses. When only 1 number is given, it applies to all sizes. Model shown is medium size.

Finished Measurements

Circumference: 18 (20, 22) inches (stretched slightly)
Height: 8 (8½, 9) inches

Materials

- Plymouth Encore Worsted (worsted weight; 75% acrylic/25% wool; 200 yds/100g per skein): 2 skeins medium brown #6002 (A)
- Plymouth Baby Alpaca Ultimo (super bulky weight; 90% alpaca/10% nylon; 109 yds/100g per skein): 1 skein white #100 (B)
- Size 10 (6mm) 16-inch circular needle
- Size 11 (8mm) 16-inch circular and double-point needles (set of 5) or size needed to obtain gauge
- Stitch marker

Gauge

12 sts and 18 rnds = 4 inches/10cm in St st using larger needle and 2 strands of A held tog.

To save time, take time to check gauge.

Pattern Notes

A is worked with two strands of yarn held together and B is worked with a single strand.

Change to double-point needles when necessary.

If using double-point needles for the entire hat, you will need a set of 5 smaller double-point needles.

Hat

Body

Using smaller circular needle and 2 strands of A held tog, cast on 54 (60, 66) sts; mark beg of rnd and join, being careful not to twist sts.

Work garter stitch (knit 1 rnd, purl 1 rnd) until piece measures 2¾ (3, 3¼) inches, ending with a purl rnd. Do not cut A.

With B, work 2 rnds garter st. Cut B, leaving an 8-inch tail.

Change to larger circular needle and A.

Rnd 1: Knit.

Rnd 2: *Sl 1, k8 (9, 10); rep from * around.

Rep Rnds 1 and 2 until body measures 4½ (4¾, 5) inches, ending with Rnd 2.

Crown

Size Small Only
Rnd 1: *K7, k2tog; rep from * around—48 sts.

Rnd 2: *S1, k7; rep from * around.

Size Medium Only
Rnd 1: *K1, k2tog, k5, ssk; rep from * around—48 sts.

Rnd 2: *Sl 1, k7; rep from * around.

Rnd 3: Knit.

Rnd 4: Rep Rnd 2.

Size Large Only
Rnd 1: *K9, k2tog; rep from * around—60 sts.

Rnd 2: *Sl 1, k9; rep from * around.

Rnd 3: *K1, k2tog, k5, ssk; rep from * around—48 sts.

Rnd 4: *Sl 1, k7; rep from * around.

Rnd 5: Knit.

Rnd 6: Rep Rnd 4.

All Sizes
Rnd 1: *K1, k2tog, k3, ssk; rep from * around—36 sts.

Rnds 2 and 4: *Sl 1, k5; rep from * around.

Rnd 3: Knit.

Rnd 5: *K1, k2tog, k1, ssk; rep from * around—24 sts.

Rnds 6 and 8: *Sl 1, k3; rep from * around.

Rnd 7: Knit.

Rnd 9: *K1, sk2p; rep from * around—12 sts.

Rnd 10: *Sl 1, k1; rep from * around.

Rnd 11: *K2tog; rep from * around—6 sts.

Cut yarn, leaving a tail at least 10 inches long. Thread tail through rem sts and pull tight to close hole in top of hat. Weave in tail on WS.

Finishing
Weave in ends. Block.

Bottom Edging

With RS facing, using smaller needle and B, pick up and knit 54 (60, 66) sts around cast-on edge; do not turn.

Bind off all sts.

Cut yarn, leaving an 8-inch tail. Use tail to join beg and end of rnds. Weave in tails invisibly along edge.

Faux Seam Lines

Using tapestry needle threaded with 2 strands of B, embroider a line of running sts following the slipped-st lines in the top half of the hat (between the decs). Beg at the center B garter st stripe, go to the top of the crown, then back down line of slip sts on opposite side ending at center stripe. Rep twice more, along rem slip-st lines. Don't pull the sts too tight when working the running st; the yarn should puff out. Work slowly and gently to avoid tangles in the yarn. ●

T!P

HOW TO

Since the body of the hat is made with two strands of yarn held together, 2 skeins are suggested for convenience. If you prefer, 1 skein has sufficient yarn to make the hat but it should first be wound into two separate balls of equal weight.

Running Stitch

Color Brick Stitch

Made with neutrals or bold colors, this hat is a crowd pleaser that looks good on either guys or gals.

....

Skill Level

◼◼◼◻ INTERMEDIATE

Sizes

Small (medium, large) to fit average child (woman, man)

Instructions are given for smallest size, with larger sizes in parentheses. When only 1 number is given, it applies to all sizes.

Finished Measurements

Circumference: 17¾ (19½, 21½) inches (slightly stretched)
Height: 7 (8, 9) inches

Materials

- Cascade Yarn Eco Cloud (Aran weight; 70% merino wool/30% alpaca; 164 yds/100g per hank): 1 hank fawn #1803 (A)
- SMC Select Tweed Deluxe (chunky weight; 54% alpaca/32% wool/ 14% polyamide; 87 yds/50g per ball): 1 ball silver natural #7116 (B)
- Size 7 (4.5mm) 16-inch circular needle
- Size 9 (5.5mm) 16-inch circular and double-point needles (set of 5) or size needed to obtain gauge
- Stitch markers, 1 in CC for beg of rnd

Gauge

18 sts and 24 rnds = 4 inches/10 cm in St st with larger needle.

To save time, take time to check gauge.

Pattern Stitches

Brick (multiple of 4 sts)
Rnd 1: With B, knit.
Rnd 2: With B, purl.
Rnds 3 and 4: With A, *k3, sl 1; rep from * around.

Rnds 5 and 6: Rep Rnds 1 and 2.
Rnds 7 and 8: With A, k1, sl 1, *k3, sl 1; rep from * to last 2 sts, k2.
Rep Rnds 1–8 for pat.

Welt
Rnds 1 and 2: With A, knit.
Rnd 3: With B, knit.
Rnd 4: With B, purl.
Rep Rnds 1–4, dec as instructed.

Pattern Notes

Change to double-point needles when necessary.

If using double-point needles for the entire hat, you will need a set of 5 smaller double-point needles.

When changing colors, do not cut yarn that's not in use.

Hat

Using smaller circular needle and A, cast on 80 (88, 96) sts; mark beg of rnd and join, being careful not to twist sts.

Rnds 1–7: *K3, p1; rep from * around.

Change to larger circular needle.

Work even in Brick pat until piece measures 5¼ (5¾, 6¼) inches, ending with Rnd 2 or 6 (4 or 8, 2 or 6).

Crown

Change to Welt pat, beg with Rnd 1 (3, 1).

Set-up rnd: *Work 8 (9, 10) sts in pat, k2tog, pm; rep from * around—72 (80, 88) sts.

Work 1 rnd even.

Dec rnd: Work to 2 sts before marker, k2tog; rep from * around—64 (72, 80) sts.

Continue in Welt pat and rep Dec rnd [every other rnd] 7 (8, 9) times, removing markers on last rnd—8 sts.

Cut yarn, leaving a tail at least 10 inches long. Thread tail through rem sts and pull tight to close hole in top of hat. Weave in tail on WS.

Weave in all other ends. Block as desired. •

Chunky Lace Beanie

Chunky yarn and an easy lace stitch make this chic design a quick project that's perfect for a last-minute gift or a treat for you.

Skill Level
◼◼◼◻ INTERMEDIATE

Sizes
Small (medium, large) to fit average child (woman, man)

Instructions are given for smallest size, with larger sizes in parentheses. When only 1 number is given, it applies to all sizes.

Finished Measurements
Circumference: 17½ (20, 22½) inches (stretched slightly)
Height: 7½ (8½, 9½) inches

Materials
- Caron Sheep(ish) (worsted weight; 70% acrylic/30% wool; 167 yds/85g per skein): 2 skeins pumpkin(ish) #0013
- Size 11 (8mm) 16-inch circular and double-point needles (set of 5) or size needed to obtain gauge

Gauge
12 sts and 16 rnds = 4 inches/10cm in St st with 2 strands held tog.

11 sts and 16 rnds = 4 inches/10cm in Lace pat with 2 strands held tog.

To save time, take time to check gauge.

Pattern Stitch
Lace (multiple of 7 sts)
Note: A chart is provided for those preferring to work pat st from a chart.
Rnds 1 and 3: Knit.
Rnd 2: *K3, [yo, p2tog] twice; rep from * around.
Rnd 4: *K3, [p2tog, yo] twice; rep from * around.
Rep Rnds 1–4 for pat.

Pattern Note
Change to double-point needles when necessary.

Hat

Body
Using circular needle and 2 strands of yarn held tog, cast on 49 (56, 63) sts; mark beg of rnd and join, being careful not to twist sts.

Knit 1 rnd.

Work Lace pat until piece measures 4 (5, 6) inches, ending with an odd-numbered rnd.

Crown
Rnd 1: *K3, p2tog, yo, p2tog; rep from * around—42 (48, 54) sts.

Rnd 2 and all even-numbered rnds: Knit.

Rnd 3: Remove marker, k1, pm for new beg of rnd; *k2, yo, p2tog, k2tog; rep from * around—35 (40, 45) sts.

Rnd 5: *K1, ssk, yo, k2tog; rep from * around—28 (32, 36) sts.

Rnd 7: *Ssk, yo, k2tog; rep from * around—21 (24, 27) sts.

Rnd 9: *K1, k2tog; rep from * around—14 (16, 18) sts.

Rnd 11: *K2tog; rep from * around—7 (8, 9) sts.

Remove marker and cut yarn, leaving a tail at least 10 inches long. Thread tail through rem sts and pull tight to close hole in top of hat. Weave in tail on WS.

Weave in all other ends. Block as desired. •

7-st rep

LACE CHART

STITCH KEY	
☐	K
○	Yo
⧄	P2tog

Zigzag Tam

"Wow! How did you do that?" Just smile when your friends ask because they won't know how much fun you had making this stylish hat.

Skill Level
■■■☐ INTERMEDIATE

Sizes
Small (medium, large) to fit average child (woman, man)

Instructions are given for smallest size, with larger sizes in parentheses. When only 1 number is given, it applies to all sizes.

Finished Measurements
Circumference (measured along bottom of band): 17½ (20, 22) inches
Height: 8 inches

Materials
- Classic Elite Magnolia (DK weight; 70% merino wool/30% silk; 120 yds/50g per ball): 1 ball each bright orchid #5495 (A), berry #5425 (B) and Persian orange #5485 (C)
- Size 4 (3.5mm) 16-inch circular needle
- Size 6 (4mm) 16-inch circular and double-point needles (set of 5) or size needed to obtain gauge
- Stitch markers, 1 in CC for beg of rnd

Gauge
20 sts and 24 rnds = 4 inches/10cm in St st with larger needle.

To save time, take time to check gauge.

Pattern Stitches
Zigzag (multiple of 14 sts)
Rnd 1: Knit.
Rnd 2: *Kfb, k4, skp, k2tog, k4, kfb; rep from * around.
Rep Rnds 1 and 2 for pat.

Body Stripe Sequence
Work [4 rnds B, 4 rnds C, 4 rnds A] twice, 4 rnds B.

Crown Stripe Sequence
Work *2 rnds C, 2 rnds A, 2 rnds B; rep from *.

Pattern Notes
If desired, place a marker after each repeat of the Zigzag pattern. The beginning-of-round marker should be a different color from the other markers.

This pattern cycles through all 3 colors. It is not necessary to cut the yarn when a stripe is finished. Let the yarn hang loose when not in use. At the end of each plain knit round (Round 1) of Zigzag pattern, pass the working yarn under the unused colors making a loop which will carry the strands up 2 rounds. When starting a new color stripe, be sure the first stitch isn't pulled too tightly.

If you want the tam to be shorter or taller, decrease or increase the number of 4-rnd body stripes. The stitch pattern for shaping the crown remains the same; revise the crown stripe sequence as necessary to maintain the established order.

Change to double-point needles when necessary. If using double-point needles for the entire hat, you will need a set of 5 smaller double-point needles.

Hat

Using smaller circular needle and A, cast on 112 (128, 140) sts; mark beg of rnd and join, being careful not to twist sts.

Work 8 rnds in k2, p2 Rib.

Inc rnd 1: *K1, kfb, p2; rep from * around—140 (160, 175) sts.

Inc rnd 2: Change to larger circular needle and B, beginning the Body Stripe Sequence; *k9 (19, 24), kfb; rep from * around—154 (168, 182) sts.

Next rnd: Work Rnd 2 of Zigzag pat.

Continue in Zigag pat and complete Body Stripe Sequence, ending with 4 rnds B.

Crown

Work 2-rnd Crown Stripe Sequence and dec as follows:

Rnd 1 and all odd-numbered rnds: Knit.

Rnd 2: *Kfb, k2, [skp] twice, [k2tog] twice, k2, kfb; rep from * around—132 (144, 156) sts.

Rnd 4: *Kfb, k3, skp, k2tog, k3, kfb; rep from * around.

Rnd 6: *Kfb, k1, [skp] twice, [k2tog] twice, k1, kfb; rep from * around—110 (120, 130) sts.

Rnd 8: *Kfb, k2, skp, k2tog, k2, kfb; rep from * around.

Rnd 10: *Kfb, [skp] twice, [k2tog] twice, kfb; rep from * around—88 (96, 104) sts.

Rnd 12: *Kfb, k1, skp, k2tog, k1, kfb; rep from * around.

Note: Pay attention to change in dec technique on Rnd 14.

Rnd 14: *Kfb, sk2p, k3tog, kfb; rep from * around—66 (72, 78) sts.

Rnd 16: *Kfb, skp, k2tog, kfb; rep from * around.

Rnd 18: *K1, skp, k2tog, k1; rep from * around—44 (48, 52) sts.

Rnd 20: Knit.

Rnd 22: *Skp, k2tog; rep from * around—22 (24, 26) sts.

Rnd 24: *K2tog; rep from * around—11 (12, 13) sts.

Rnd 25: *K2tog; rep from * to last 1 (0, 1) st(s), k1 (0, 1)—6 (6, 7) sts.

Remove marker and cut yarn, leaving tail at least 10 inches long. Thread tail through rem sts and pull tight to close hole in top of hat. Weave in tail on WS.

Weave in all other ends. Block as desired. ●

T!P

HOW TO

Hat is designed to be somewhat loose and slouchy. For a more traditional fit, make a size smaller or use smaller needles. Alternatively, if a tighter fit is desired, an elastic cord can be run through the first row of ribbing on the WS.

Tailored Cloche

Elegant simplicity is the perfect description for this hat. You'll also find the clever construction technique an interesting addition to your knitting skills.

Skill Level

■■■□ INTERMEDIATE

Sizes
Small (medium, large) to fit average child (woman, man)

Instructions are given for smallest size, with larger sizes in parentheses. When only 1 number is given, it applies to all sizes. Model shown is medium size.

Finished Measurements
Circumference: 18 (20, 22) inches
Height: 8 (8½, 9) inches

Materials
- Universal Yarn Deluxe Worsted (worsted weight; 100% wool; 220 yds/100g per skein): 1 hank kombu green #12169 (A)
- Universal Yarn/Wisdom Yarns Poems (worsted weight; 100% wool; 109 yds/50g per hank): 2 skeins la lavande #588 (B)
- Size 7 (4.5mm) 16-inch circular and double-point needles (set of 5) or size needed to obtain gauge
- Size 8 (5mm) 16-inch circular needle
- Round stitch markers
- Locking stitch marker

4 MEDIUM

Gauge
18 sts and 24 rnds = 4 inches/10cm in St st with smaller needles.

To save time, take time to check gauge.

Pattern Note
Change to double-point needles when necessary. Making the hat with only double-point needles is not recommended.

Hat

Brim
With smaller circular needle and A, cast on 80 (90, 100) sts; mark beg of rnd and join, being careful not to twist sts.

Rnds 1–5: Knit.

Rnd 6 (color-change rnd): Change to larger needle and B; place locking marker in first st of rnd; purl around.

Note: After completing Rnd 6, look at the sts. You will see the bottom of the purl st made with B making small loops or bumps, 1 for each st, below the knit st made with A. Later, these B-loops will be used to join the 2 layers of the brim tog.

Work even, purling every rnd until piece measures approx 3 (3¼, 3½) inches from marked color-change rnd.

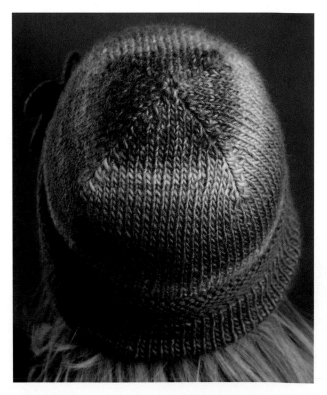

Joining rnd: *P1, pick up st from below and knit through back loop; rep from * around—160 (180, 200) sts. Remove locking stitch marker at the end of this rnd. For additional instruction on the joining round, see "How to Join the Brim."

Dec rnd: *K2tog; rep from * around—80 (90, 100) sts.

Body

Change to smaller needle; knit all rnds until piece measures 6¼ (6¾, 7¼) inches from brim-fold edge, and on last rnd, dec 0 (2, 4) sts evenly around—80 (88, 96) sts.

Crown

Set-up rnd: [K2tog, k16 (18, 20), ssk, pm] 4 times—72 (80, 88) sts.

Knit 1 rnd.

Dec rnd: [K2tog, knit to 2 sts before marker, ssk] 4 times—64 (72, 80) sts.

Rep Dec rnd [every other rnd] 7 (8, 9) times, removing markers on last rnd—8 sts.

Cut yarn, leaving a tail at least 10 inches long. Thread tail through rem sts and pull tight to close hole in top of hat. Weave in tail on WS.

Weave in all other ends. Block as desired.

Finishing
4-st I-Cord Bow (optional)

With A and smaller needle, cast on 4 sts. Do not turn.

Slip sts back to LH needle, k4, do not turn; rep from * until cord measures approx 12 inches.

Bind off and cut yarn. Weave tail invisibly into cord. Block as desired.

Tie I-cord into a bow and tack or pin onto the hat in the desired location. ●

Join Brim

Fold the purl section in half (with the purl sts to the inside) and hold it so that the color-change rnd is just above the needle, with the 5 rnds of A folded down in front.

Locate the bottom loops or bumps made by the purl sts in Rnd 6. You will purl 1 st as usual from the needle and then knit the purl loop from the color-change rnd.

To knit, pick up the purl loop by inserting the LH needle from the back to the front.

The first loop will be adjacent to the marked st. You

may find it easier to use the RH needle to pick up the loop, and then transfer it to the LH needle. The loop (or st), will be twisted on the LH needle so knit this st through the back loop.

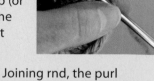

As you work across the Joining rnd, the purl section (yarn B) section will fold in half with the knit sts facing out.

Remember to move the yarn back and forth between the needles just as you would if you were knitting a traditional k1, p1 rib.

Seed Stitch Newsboy

Show some attitude! This newsboy hat is rich in detail and is a fun project for working on new skills like the short rows used to make the brim.

Skill Level
■■■□ INTERMEDIATE

Sizes
Small (medium, large) to fit average child (woman, man)

Instructions are given for smallest size, with larger sizes in parentheses. When only 1 number is given, it applies to all sizes.

Finished Measurements
Circumference: 17½ (20, 22½) inches
Height: 6¾ (7½, 8¼) inches

Materials
- Patons Shetland Chunky Tweeds (chunky weight; 72% acrylic/ 25% wool/3% viscose; 125 yds/85g per ball): 1 (2, 2) balls sea ice tweeds #67128
- Size 7 (4.5mm) 16-inch circular needle
- Size 9 (5.5mm) 16-inch circular and double-point needles (set of 5) or size needed to obtain gauge
- Round stitch marker
- Locking stitch marker
- Ultra firm interfacing to stiffen brim (Pellon Peltex 71, available in fabric stores, was used in model)

5 BULKY

Gauge
16 sts and 24 rnds = 4 inches/10cm in seed stitch with larger needle.

To save time, take time to check gauge.

Pattern Stitch
Body pat (multiple of 10 sts)
Rnd 1: *K2, [p1, k1] 4 times; rep from * around.
Rnd 2: *Sl 1, [p1, k1] 4 times, p1; rep from * around.
Rep Rnds 1 and 2 for pat.

Pattern Notes
If using circular needle for body, change to double-point needles when necessary.

If using double-point needles for the entire hat, you will need a set of 5 smaller double-point needles.

See tutorial for how to work short rows.

Hat
With smaller circular needle, cast on 70 (80, 90) sts; mark beg of rnd and join, being careful not to twist sts. Using locking st marker, mark the 35th (40th, 45th) st of rnd for midpoint of brim.

Work 5 rnds in k1, p1 rib.

Body
Change to larger needle.

Work 2-rnd Body pat until piece measures 4½ (5¼, 6) inches, ending with Rnd 2.

Crown
Rnd 1: *K2, p1, k1, p3tog, k1, p1, k1; rep from * around—56 (64, 72) sts.

Rnd 2: *Sl 1, [p1, k1] 3 times, p1; rep from * around.

Rnd 3: *K2, [p1, k1] 3 times; rep from * around.

Rnd 4: *Sl 1, p1, k1, p3tog, k1, p1; rep from * around—42 (48, 54) sts.

Rnd 5: *K2, [p1, k1] twice; rep from * around.

Rnd 6: *Sl 1, [p1, k1] twice, p1; rep from * around.

Rnd 7: *K2, p3tog, k1; rep from * around—28 (32, 36) sts.

Rnd 8: *Sl 1, p1, k1, p1; rep from * around.

Rnd 9: *K2, p1, k1; rep from * around.

Rnd 10: *K1, p3tog; rep from * around—14, (16, 18) sts.

Rnd 11: Knit.

Rnd 12: *Ssk; rep from * around—7 (8, 9) sts.

Remove marker and cut yarn, leaving a tail at least 10 inches long. Thread tail through rem sts and pull tight to close hole in top of hat. Weave in tail on WS.

Weave in all other ends. Block as desired.

Brim
Count 17 (19, 21) sts to right of marked center-brim st. Beg at this point, pick up and knit 34 (38, 42) sts across cast-on edge, picking up 1 st in each cast-on st.

Row 1 (RS): K31 (34, 37), W&T.

Row 2: P28 (30, 32), W&T.

Row 3: K25 (27, 29), W&T.

Row 4: P22 (24, 26) W&T.

Row 5: K19 (21, 23), W&T.

Row 6: P16 (18, 20), W&T.

Row 7: K13 (15, 17), W&T.

Row 8: P10 (12, 14), W&T.

Row 9: K22 (25, 28), hiding all wraps.

Row 10: Purl across, hiding all wraps.

Row 11: K22 (25, 28), W&T.

Row 12: P10 (12, 14), W&T.

Note: Hide wrap when you come to it on following rows.

Row 13: K13 (15, 17), W&T.

Row 14: P16 (18, 20), W&T.

Row 15: K19 (21, 23), W&T.

Row 16: P22 (24, 26), W&T.

Row 17: K25 (27, 29), W&T.

Row 18: P28 (30, 32), W&T.

Row 19: K31 (34, 37).

Row 20: Purl across.

Bind off.

Fold brim in half along long, curved edge. The bound-off edge of the lower brim should just slightly overlap the cast-on edge of the hat. Lightly block the brim.

Use the folded brim as a template to trace and cut a crescent shape from the interfacing. Snip the sharp ends off both sides of the interfacing so it won't poke through the hat sts. Insert the interfacing between the upper and lower halves of the brim, then sew the lower brim to the WS of hat.

Weave in all ends and block as desired. •

Short Rows: Wrap & Turn (W&T)

Short rows are used to create shaping by knitting across some, but not all, of the stitches in a row before turning to work the next row. Numerous short rows placed close together create an arc which is how the shaping for the hat brim is accomplished. In order to avoid holes in the knitting where the short row is turned, the turning stitch must be wrapped. This is where the term wrap and turn (W&T) comes from. When it comes time to work across the full row, the wrap at the base of the stitch must be knit or purled together with the stitch on the needle. This will "hide" the wrap.

Wrapping Stitch
Knit side

Knit across the row to the turning stitch. Keeping the yarn in back, slip the next stitch purlwise. Move the yarn between the needles to the front and return the slipped stitch to the left-hand needle. Finally, move the yarn between the needles to the back. Turn the piece and work the next row as indicated.

Purl side

Purl across the row to the turning stitch. Keeping the yarn in front, slip the next stitch purlwise. Move the yarn between the needles to the back and return the slipped stitch to the left-hand needle. Finally, move the yarn between the needles to the front. Turn the piece and work the next row as indicated.

Hiding Wraps
Knit side

Knit the wrap and stitch on the needle together by inserting the right-hand needle knitwise under the wrap and into the stitch and knitting the two loops together.

Purl side

First, pick the wrap by inserting the right-hand needle from behind into the back loop of the wrap and placing it on the left-hand needle. Purl the wrap and the stitch together.

Purl the wrap and the stitch together.

Slouchy Beanie

A simple beanie pattern receives an updated boho look with a longer length and gathered crown. This is a perfect pattern for showcasing beautiful luxury yarn.

Skill Level
◼◼◻◻ EASY

Sizes
Small (medium, large) to fit average child (woman, man)

Instructions are given for smallest size, with larger sizes in parentheses. When only 1 number is given, it applies to all sizes.

Finished Measurements
Circumference: 18 (20, 22) inches, measured approx 4 inches above cast-on rnd
Height: 10 (11, 11½) inches

Materials
- Plymouth Yarn Juli (chunky weight; 63% alpaca/32% nylon/5% polyester; 101 yds/50g per ball): 2 balls light brown #2
- Size 9 (5.5 mm) 16-inch circular needle
- Size 10½ (6.5mm) 16-inch circular and double-point needles (set of 5) or size needed to obtain gauge
- Stitch marker
- 1 (1-inch) button Glamour Gems #5214 from Blumenthal Lansing (optional)
- Sewing needle and thread for attaching button (optional)

Gauge
15½ sts and 20 rnds = 4 inches/10cm in St st with larger needle.

To save time, take time to check gauge.

Pattern Notes
Change to double-point needles when necessary.

If using double-point needles for the entire hat, you will need a set of 5 smaller double-point needles.

Hat
Using smaller circular needle, cast on 66 (78, 84) sts; mark beg of rnd and join, being careful not to twist sts.

Work 11 rnds in k3, p3 rib.

Next rnd: Change to larger needle; knit and inc 4 (0, 2) sts evenly around—70 (78, 86) sts.

Work even in St st (knit all rnds) until piece measures 9 (10, 10½) inches.

Crown
Rnd 1: K33 (37, 41), k2tog; rep from * once—68 (76, 84) sts.

Rnd 2: *K2, k2tog; rep from * around—51 (57, 63) sts.

Rnd 3: *K1, k2tog; rep from * around—34 (38, 42) sts.

Rnd 4: *K2tog; rep from * around—17 (19, 21) sts.

Rnd 5: *K2tog; rep from * to last st, k1—9 (10, 11) sts.

Remove marker and cut yarn, leaving a tail at least 10 inches long. Thread tail through rem sts and pull tight to close hole in top of hat. Weave in tail on WS.

Weave in all other ends. Block as desired. If desired, sew button to top of hat. ●

Folk Art

This hat is a delight to wear and fun to knit. The slip stitch pattern is easy and a great way to show off your color sense.

Skill Level

◼◼◼◻ INTERMEDIATE

Sizes

Small (medium, large) to fit average child (woman, man)

Instructions are given for smallest size, with larger sizes in parentheses. When only 1 number is given, it applies to all sizes.

Finished Measurements

Circumference: 17¾ (20, 22¼) inches
Height (with bottom edge unrolled):
12 (12½, 13) inches, not including pompom

Materials

- Dream in Color Classy (worsted weight; 100% merino wool; 250 yds/113g per hank): 1 hank each black parade (A), punky fuchsia (B), visual purple (C), go go grassy (D) and summer sky (E)
- Size 7 (4.5mm) 16-inch circular and double-point needles (set of 5) or size needed to obtain gauge
- Stitch marker
- Pompom maker for 2-inch pompom (optional)

4 MEDIUM

Gauge

18 sts and 28 rnds = 4 inches/10cm in St st.

To save time, take time to check gauge.

Pattern Stitches

Textured Pat (even number of sts)
Rnd 1: Change color; knit 1 rnd.
Rnds 2 and 3: Purl 2 rnds.
Rnds 4–6: With A, knit 3 rnds.
Rnds 7 and 8: Change color; knit 2 rnds.
Rnd 9: Change color; *k1, sl 1; rep from * around.
Rnd 10: *P1, sl 1; rep from * around.
Rnds 11 and 12: Change color, knit 2 rnds.
Rnds 13–15: With A, knit 3 rnds.
Rep Rnds 1–15 for pat, changing colors as per Stripe Sequence.

Stripe Sequence

Pat Rep 1: 3 rnds B, 3 rnds A, 2 rnds C, 2 rnds D, 2 rnds E, 3 rnds A.
Pat Rep 2: 3 rnds C, 3 rnds A, 2 rnds D, 2 rnds E, 2 rnds B, 3 rnds A.
Pat Rep 3: 3 rnds D, 3 rnds A, 2 rnds E, 2 rnds B, 2 rnds C, 3 rnds A.
Pat Rep 4: 3 rnds E, 3 rnds A, 2 rnds B, 2 rnds C, 2 rnds D, 3 rnds A.

Pattern Notes

Change to double-point needles when necessary.

Carry A along during Stripe Sequence; when starting stripe with A, do not pull yarn too tightly. Cut all other colors after each stripe.

Hat

Body

With circular needle and A, cast on 80 (90, 100) sts; mark beg of rnd and join, being careful not to twist sts.

Work in St st (knit all rnds) until piece measures 1 inch.

Work 4 reps of 15-rnd Textured pat, working each rep's Stripe Sequence as indicated.

With B, knit 2 rnds.

With A, knit 3 rnds.

With C, knit 2 rnds.

With A, knit 3 rnds.

With D, knit 2 rnds.

Sizes Medium (Large) Only
With A, knit 3 rnds.

With E, knit 2 rnds.

All Sizes
Cut all colors but A.

With A, work even in St st until body measures approx 10 (10½, 11) inches from unrolled cast-on edge, and on last rnd, dec 2 (0, 4) sts evenly around—78 (90, 96) sts.

Crown

Rnd 1: *K4, k2tog; rep from * around—65 (75, 80) sts.

Rnds 2, 4, 6 and 8: Knit.

Rnd 3: *K3, k2tog; rep from * around—52 (60, 64) sts.

Rnd 5: *K2, k2tog; rep from * around—39 (45, 48) sts.

Rnd 7: *K1, k2tog; rep from * around—26 (30, 32) sts.

Rnd 9: *K2tog; rep from * around—13 (15, 16) sts.

Rnd 10: *K2tog; rep from * to last 1 (1, 0) st(s), k1 (1, 0)—7 (8, 8) sts.

Cut yarn, leaving a tail at least 10 inches long. Thread tail through rem sts and pull tight to close hole in top of hat. Weave in tail on WS.

Weave in all other ends. Block as desired.

Pompom

Using all 5 colors, make a 2-inch pompom using pompom maker or as follows:

Cut two cardboard circles 2 inches in diameter. Cut a hole in the center of each circle, about ½-inch in diameter. Thread a tapestry needle with long strands of all 5 colors. Holding both circles together, insert needle through center hole, over the outside edge, through center again until entire circle is covered and center hole is filled (thread more yarn as needed).

With sharp scissors, cut yarn between the two circles all around the circumference.

Using two 12-inch strands of yarn, slip yarn between circles and overlap yarn ends 2 or 3 times to prevent knot from slipping, pull tightly and tie into a firm knot. Remove cardboard and fluff out pompom by rolling it between your hands. Trim even with scissors, leaving tying ends for attaching pompom to hat.

Attach pompom securely to top of hat. ●

T!P
HOW TO

It is not necessary to cut A when other colors are being used. Let the yarn hang loose when not in use. When knitting the next stripe with A, be sure the first stitch isn't pulled too tightly. The other colors should be cut when not in use and the ends woven in.

Stocking Cap for Little Ones

Add some playfulness to this adorable stocking cap with clever spiral shaping lines.

Sizes

Child's 0–3 (3–18, 18–24) months

Instructions are given for smallest size, with larger sizes in parentheses. When only 1 number is given, it applies to all sizes.

Finished Measurements

Circumference: 12 (14, 16) inches
Length: 10 (10½, 11¼) inches

Materials

- Plymouth Worsted Merino Superwash (worsted weight; 100% merino wool; 218 yds/100g per skein): 1 skein turquoise #56
- Size 6 (4mm) 12- (12-, 16-) inch circular needle
- Size 7 (4.5mm) 12- (12-, 16-) inch circular and double-point needles (set of 5) or size needed to obtain gauge
- Stitch markers, 1 in CC for beg of rnd

Gauge

20 sts and 28 rnds = 4 inches/10cm in St st with larger needle.

To save time, take time to check gauge.

Special Abbreviation

Make 1 Right (M1R): Insert LH needle from back to front under horizontal bar between st on RH needle and st on LH needle. Insert RH needle into front of the strand on the LH needle, giving the strand a twist. K1 in resulting loop.

Pattern Stitch

Spiral (multiple of 10 sts)
Rnd 1: *K8, k2tog, M1R; rep from * around.
Rnd 2 and all even-numbered rnds: Knit.
Rnd 3: *K7, k2tog, M1R, k1; rep from * around.
Rnd 5: *K6, k2tog, M1R, k2; rep from * around.
Rnd 7: *K5, k2tog, M1R, k3; rep from * around.
Rnd 9: *K4, k2tog, M1R, k4; rep from * around.
Rnd 11: *K3, k2tog, M1R, k5; rep from * around.
Rnd 13: *K2, k2tog, M1R, k6; rep from * around.
Rnd 15: *K1, k2tog, M1R, k7; rep from * around.
Rnd 17: *K2tog, M1R, k8; rep from * around.
Rnd 18: Knit to last 9 sts, pm for new beg of rnd; remove previous marker on next rnd.
Rep Rnds 1–18 for pat.

Pattern Note

Work smaller hats using shorter circular needles or work entire hat with double-point needles. If using double-point needles for the entire hat, you will need a set of 5 smaller double-point needles. If using circular needle, change to double-point needles when necessary.

Hat

Using larger circular needle, cast on 60 (70, 80) sts; mark beg of rnd and join, being careful not to twist sts.

Knit 3 rnds.

Change to smaller needle; work 2 rnds in k1, p1 rib.

Change to larger needle and knit 1 rnd.

Work Rnds 7–18 (1–18, 13–18) of Spiral pat.

Work complete 18-rnd Spiral pat 1 (1, 2) time(s) more.

Crown

Set-up rnd: *K8, k2tog, pm; rep from * around— 54 (63, 72) sts.

Knit 2 rnds.

Dec rnd: Knit to 2 sts before marker, k2tog; rep from * around—48 (56, 64) sts.

Continuing in St st, rep Dec rnd [every 3 rnds] twice more, then [every 4 rnds] 5 times—6 (7, 8) sts.

Removing all markers but beg of rnd marker, knit 3 rnds.

Last rnd: Remove beg of rnd marker; [k2tog] 2 (3, 4) times, k2 (1, 0)—4 sts.

Cut yarn, leaving a tail at least 10 inches long. Thread tail through rem sts and pull tight to close hole in top of hat. Weave in tail on WS.

Weave in all other ends. Block as desired. ●

Baby Earflap

Who says the big kids should have all the fun? This darling hat will keep babies warm and happy and give them a bit of attitude as well.

Skill Level
■■□□ EASY

Sizes
Child's 0–3 (3–18, 18–24) months

Instructions are given for smallest size, with larger sizes in parentheses. When only 1 number is given, it applies to all sizes.

Finished Measurements
Circumference: 12 (14, 16) inches
Height: 6¾ (7, 8) inches (not including earflaps or I-cord knot on top)

Materials
- Berroco Comfort (worsted weight; 50% nylon/50% acrylic; 210 yds/100g per ball): 1 ball Sanibel Island #9837
- Size 7 (4.5mm) 12- (12-, 16-) inch circular and double-point needles (set of 5) or size needed to obtain gauge
- Size 5 (3.75mm) 12- (12-, 16-) inch circular and double-point needles (set of 3)
- Stitch markers, 1 in CC for beg of rnd

Gauge
20 sts and 28 rnds = 4 inches/10cm in St st with larger needle.

To save time, take time to check gauge.

Pattern Note
Work smaller hats using shorter circular needles or work entire hat with double-point needles. If using double-point needles for the entire hat, you will need a set of 5 smaller double-point needles. If using circular needle for body, change to double-point needles when necessary.

Earflaps
Make 2

Using smaller dpn, cast on 6 sts.

Rows 1 and 2: Knit.

Row 3 (RS): Kfb, knit to last 2 sts, kfb, k1—8 sts.

Rows 4–6: Knit.

Rep [Rows 3–6] 4 (5, 6) times—16 (18, 20) sts.

Work even in garter st until piece measures 2¼ (2½, 2¾) inches.

Cut yarn and set aside on spare dpn.

Body
Begin by casting on 3 separate sets of sts as follows:

With smaller circular needle, cast on 5 (6, 7) sts, cut yarn; leaving first set of sts in place, cast on 18 (22, 26) sts, cut yarn; cast on 5 (6, 7) sts, do not cut yarn, turn.

Set-up rnd: K5 (6, 7), knit across first earflap, k18 (22, 26), knit across second earflap, k5 (6, 7); mark beg of rnd and join, being careful not to twist st—60 (70, 80) sts.

Work in garter st (purl 1 rnd, knit 1 rnd) until piece measures 1 (1, 1¼) inch(es) from body cast-on.

Change to larger circular needle and St st (knit all rnds).

Inc 0 (2, 0) sts on first rnd and dec 4 (0, 0) sts on last rnd, work in St st until body measures approx 4½ (5, 5½) inches—56 (72, 80) sts.

Crown
Set-up rnd: *K5 (7, 8), k2tog, pm; rep from * around—48 (64, 72) sts.

Knit 1 rnd.

Dec rnd: *Knit to 2 sts before marker, k2tog; rep from * around—40 (56, 64) sts.

Continue in St st and rep Dec rnd [every other rnd] 4 (6, 7) times—8 sts.

Next rnd: Removing all markers, k2tog around—4 sts.

4-Stitch I-Cord
Transfer 4 sts to 1 dpn with yarn coming from st furthest left on needle; do not turn.

*Bring yarn around back of dpn to beg row; k4, do not turn; slip sts back to LH needle; rep from * until I-cord measures approx 3 inches or desired length.

Bind off and cut yarn.

Weave tail into center of I-cord. Tie into knot.

Weave in all ends and block as desired. ●

T!P

HOW TO

If you don't wish to make the I-cord knot on top, then end when 8 sts rem. Remove marker and cut yarn, leaving a tail at least 10 inches long. Thread tail through the rem sts and pull tight to close hole in top of hat. Weave in tail on WS.

Basic Hat for Little Ones

Knitted flowers with button centers transform this simple hat into an adorable fashion statement.

. . . .

Skill Level

 EASY

Sizes

Baby (Toddler, Child)

Instructions are given for smallest size, with larger sizes in parentheses. When only 1 number is given, it applies to all sizes.

Finished Measurements

Circumference: 14 (16, 18) inches
Height (with bottom edge unrolled):
7 (7¾, 8½) inches

Materials

- Berroco Vintage (worsted weight; 50% acrylic/40% wool/10% nylon; 217 yds/100g per hank): 1 hank each gingham #5120 (A) and dewberry #5167 (B)
- Size 7 (4.5mm) 12- (12-, 16-) inch circular and double-point needles (set of 5) or size needed to obtain gauge
- Stitch marker
- T-pins
- 7 (½-inch) buttons Confetti #3281 from Blumenthal Lansing
- Sewing thread to coordinate with buttons
- Sewing needle

Gauge

20 sts and 28 rnds = 4 inches/10cm in St st.

To save time, take time to check the gauge.

HOW TO

T!P

Flowers are optional. If omitting flowers on the bottom edge, add approximately 1 inch to the length before crown shaping.

Pattern Note

Work smaller hats using shorter circular needles or work entire hat with double-point needles. If using circular needle for body, change to double-point needles when necessary.

Hat

Using circular needle and A, cast on 60 (70, 80) sts; mark beg of rnd and join, being careful not to twist sts.

Work even in St st (knit all rnds) until piece measures 4½ (5, 5½) inches from unrolled cast-on edge and on last rnd, dec 4 (6, 0) sts evenly around—56 (64, 80) sts.

Crown

Set-up rnd: K5 (6, 8), k2tog, pm; rep from * around—48 (56, 72) sts.

Knit 1 rnd.

Dec rnd: *Knit to 2 sts before marker, k2tog; rep from * around—40 (48, 64) sts.

Rep Dec rnd [every other rnd] 4 (5, 7) times, ending with a Dec rnd—8 sts.

Cut yarn, leaving a tail at least 10 inches long. Thread tail through rem sts and pull tight to close hole in top of hat. Weave in tail on WS.

Weave in all other ends. Block as desired.

Flowers
Make 7

With B, cast on 37 sts, leaving a 10-inch tail.

Row 1 (RS): *K1, yo, k5, pass 2nd, 3rd, 4th and 5th sts over the first st (closest to the RH needle tip) and off the end of the needle; rep from * to last st, k1—19 sts.

Row 2: P1, *p3tog; rep from * to end—7 sts.

Row 3: K1, *k2tog; rep from * to end—4 sts.

Row 4: Without turning needle, pass 2nd, 3rd and 4th sts over first st on needle—1 st.

Cut yarn, leaving a tail at least 10 inches long and pull through last st to finish.

Use yarn from cast-on to tack last petal in place slightly overlapping first petal. Weave in end used to tack petals but leave center end in place (it will be used for attaching flower to hat). Block flowers.

Finishing

Divide the hat edge evenly into 6 sections and mark each with a T-pin. Unroll the bottom edge of the hat and pin the flower in place at each marked point. The center of the flower should be ½ inch above the cast-on edge.

Using the tail from the center, tack the flower securely into place on the hat.

Knot the end on the WS of the hat and weave in ends.

Place button in center of flower and attach using sewing thread.

Attach flower and button to top of hat in same manner. ●

Hugs & Kisses

Wrap your favorite little one with a ring of hugs and kisses—cables that is!

Skill Level

◼◼◼◻ INTERMEDIATE

Sizes

Baby (Toddler, Child)

Instructions are given for smallest size, with larger sizes in parentheses. When only 1 number is given, it applies to all sizes.

Finished Measurements

Circumference: 14 (16, 18) inches
Height: 6¾ (7¼, 8) inches (not including earflaps)

Materials

- Plymouth Dreambaby DK (DK weight; 50% acrylic microfiber/50% nylon; 183 yds/50g per ball): 1 ball orange #142
- Size 4 (3.5mm) 12- (12-, 16-) inch circular needle
- Size 6 (4mm) 12- (12-, 16-) inch circular and double-point needles (set of 5) or size needed to obtain gauge
- Cable needle
- Stitch marker

Gauge

22 sts and 30 rnds = 4 inches/10cm in St st with larger needle.

To save time, take time to check gauge.

Special Abbreviations

Make 1 Right (M1R): Insert LH needle from back to front under horizontal bar between st on RH needle and st on LH needle. Insert RH needle into front of strand on LH needle, giving strand a twist. K1 in resulting loop.

Make 1 Left (M1L): Insert LH needle from front to back under horizontal bar between st on RH needle and st on LH needle. Insert RH needle into back of strand on LH needle, giving strand a twist. K1 in resulting loop.

2 over 2 Right Cross (2/2 RC): Sl 2 sts to cn and hold in back; k2, k2 from cn.

2 over 2 Left Cross (2/2 LC): Sl 2 sts to cn and hold in front; k2, k2 from cn.

2 over 2 Right Cross Decrease (2/2 RC Dec): Sl 2 sts to cn and hold in back; k2tog next 2 sts on LH needle; ssk sts on cn—4-st cable has been decreased to 2 sts.

2 over 2 Left Cross Decrease (2/2 LC Dec): Sl 2 sts to cn and hold in front; k2tog next 2 sts on LH needle; ssk sts on cn—4-st cable has been decreased to 2 sts.

Pattern Stitch

Note: A chart is provided for those preferring to work pat st from a chart.
Cable (multiple of 20 sts + 10)
Rnd 1: *K8, p2; rep from * around.
Rnd 2: *2/2 RC, 2/2 LC, p2, 2/2 LC, 2/2 RC, p2; rep from * to last 10 sts, 2/2 RC, 2/2 LC, p2.
Rnds 3–5: Rep Rnd 1.
Rnd 6: *2/2 LC, 2/2 RC, p2, 2/2 RC, 2/2 LC, p2; rep from * to last 10 sts, 2/2 LC, 2/2 RC, p2.
Rnds 7–9: Rep Rnd 1.
Rnd 10: Rep Rnd 6.

Pattern Note

Work smaller hats using shorter circular needles or work entire hat with double-point needles. If using double-point needles for the entire hat, you will need a set of 5 smaller double-point needles. If using circular needle for body, change to double-point needles when necessary.

Hat

Using smaller circular needle, cast on 66 (78, 90) sts. Mark beg of rnd and join, being careful not to twist sts.

Work 8 rnds in k4, p2 rib.

Inc rnd: *[K1, M1R] twice, k1, M1L, kfb, p2; rep from * around—110 (130, 150) sts.

Change to larger circular needle and work 10-rnd Cable pat.

Work 3 rnds in k8, p2 rib.

Dec rnd: *2/2 RC Dec, 2/2 LC Dec, k2, 2/2 LC Dec, 2/2 RC Dec, k2; rep from * to last 10 sts, 2/2 RC Dec, 2/2 LC Dec, k2—66 (78, 90) sts.

Work even in St st (knit all rnds) until piece measures 4½ (5, 5½) inches, and on last rnd, dec 2 (6, 2) sts evenly around—64 (72, 88) sts.

Crown

Set-up rnd: *K6 (7, 9), k2tog, pm; rep from * around—56 (64, 80) sts.

Knit 1 rnd.

Dec rnd: *Knit to 2 sts before marker, k2tog; rep from * around—48 (56, 72) sts.

Rep Dec rnd [every other rnd] 5 (6, 8) times—8 sts.

Remove marker and cut yarn, leaving a tail at least 10 inches long. Thread tail through rem sts and pull tight to close hole in top of hat. Weave in tail on WS.

Weave in all other ends. Block as desired. •

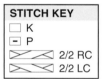

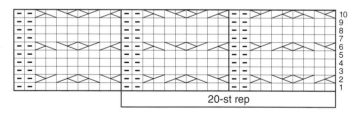

CABLE CHART

General Information

Abbreviations & Symbols

[ ] work instructions within brackets as many times as directed

( ) work instructions within parentheses in the place directed

** repeat instructions following the asterisks as directed

* repeat instructions following the single asterisk as directed

" inch(es)

approx approximately
beg begin/begins/beginning
CC contrasting color
ch chain stitch
cm centimeter(s)
cn cable needle
dec(s) decrease/decreases/ decreasing
dpn(s) double-point needle(s)
g gram(s)
inc(s) increase/increases/ increasing

k knit
k2tog knit 2 stitches together
kfb knit in front and back
kwise knitwise
LH left hand
m meter(s)
M1 make one stitch
MC main color
mm millimeter(s)
oz ounce(s)
p purl
p2tog purl 2 stitches together
pat(s) pattern(s)
pm place marker
psso pass slipped stitch over
pwise purlwise
rem remain/remains/remaining
rep(s) repeat(s)
rev St st reverse stockinette stitch
RH right hand
rnd(s) rounds
RS right side

skp slip, knit, pass slipped stitch over—1 stitch decreased
sk2p slip 1, knit 2 together, pass slipped stitch over the knit 2 together—2 stitches decreased
sl slip
sl 1 kwise slip 1 knitwise
sl 1 pwise slip 1 purlwise
sl st slip stitch(es)
ssk slip, slip, knit these 2 stitches together—a decrease
st(s) stitch(es)
St st stockinette stitch
tbl through back loop(s)
tog together
WS wrong side
wyib with yarn in back
wyif with yarn in front
yd(s) yard(s)
yfwd yarn forward
yo (yo's) yarn over(s)

Skill Levels

BEGINNER

Beginner projects for first-time knitters using basic stitches. Minimal shaping.

EASY

Easy projects using basic stitches, repetitive stitch patterns, simple color changes and simple shaping and finishing.

INTERMEDIATE

Intermediate projects with a variety of stitches, mid-level shaping and finishing.

EXPERIENCED

Experienced projects using advanced techniques and stitches, detailed shaping and refined finishing.

Standard Yarn Weight System
Categories of yarn, gauge ranges and recommended needle sizes.

Yarn Weight Symbol & Category Names	1 SUPER FINE	2 FINE	3 LIGHT	4 MEDIUM	5 BULKY	6 SUPER BULKY
Type of Yarns in Category	Sock, Fingering, Baby	Sport, Baby	DK, Light Worsted	Worsted, Afghan, Aran	Chunky, Craft, Rug	Bulky, Roving
Knit Gauge Range* in Stockinette Stitch to 4 inches	27–32 sts	23–26 sts	21–24 sts	16–20 sts	12–15 sts	6–11 sts
Recommended Needle in Metric Size Range	2.25–3.25mm	3.25–3.75mm	3.75–4.5mm	4.5–5.5mm	5.5–8mm	8mm and larger
Recommended Needle U.S. Size Range	1 to 3	3 to 5	5 to 7	7 to 9	9 to 11	11 and larger

* **GUIDELINES ONLY:** The above reflect the most commonly used gauges and needle sizes for specific yarn categories.

Inches Into Millimeters & Centimeters
All measurements are rounded off slightly.

inches	mm	cm	inches	cm	inches	cm	inches	cm
⅛	3	0.3	5	12.5	21	53.5	38	96.5
¼	6	0.6	5½	14	22	56.0	39	99.0
⅜	10	1.0	6	15.0	23	58.5	40	101.5
½	13	1.3	7	18.0	24	61.0	41	104.0
⅝	15	1.5	8	20.5	25	63.5	42	106.5
¾	20	2.0	9	23.0	26	66.0	43	109.0
⅞	22	2.2	10	25.5	27	68.5	44	112.0
1	25	2.5	11	28.0	28	71.0	45	114.5
1¼	32	3.2	12	30.5	29	73.5	46	117.0
1½	38	3.8	13	33.0	30	76.0	47	119.5
1¾	45	4.5	14	35.5	31	79.0	48	122.0
2	50	5.0	15	38.0	32	81.5	49	124.5
2½	65	6.5	16	40.5	33	84.0	50	127.0
3	75	7.5	17	43.0	34	86.5		
3½	90	9.0	18	46.0	35	89.0		
4	100	10.0	19	48.5	36	91.5		
4½	115	11.5	20	51.0	37	94.0		

Knitting Basics

Cast-On

Leaving an end about an inch long for each stitch to be cast on, make a slip knot on the right needle.

Place the thumb and index finger of your left hand between the yarn ends with the long yarn end over your thumb, and the strand from the skein over your index finger. Close your other fingers over the strands to hold them against your palm. Spread your thumb and index fingers apart and draw the yarn into a "V."

Place the needle in front of the strand around your thumb and bring it underneath this strand. Carry the needle over and under the strand on your index finger.

Draw through loop on thumb.

Drop the loop from your thumb and draw up the strand to form a stitch on the needle.

Repeat until you have cast on the number of stitches indicated in the pattern. Remember to count the beginning slip knot as a stitch.

Cable Cast-On

This type of cast-on is used when adding stitches in the middle or at the end of a row.

Make a slip knot on the left needle. Knit a stitch in this knot and place it on the left needle. Insert the right needle between the last two stitches on the left needle. Knit a stitch and place it on the left needle. Repeat for each stitch needed.

Knit (k)

Insert tip of right needle from front to back in next stitch on left needle.

Bring yarn under and over the tip of the right needle.

Pull yarn loop through the stitch with right needle point.

Slide the stitch off the left needle. The new stitch is on the right needle.

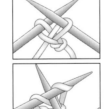

Purl (p)

With yarn in front, insert tip of right needle from back to front through next stitch on the left needle.

Bring yarn around the right needle counterclockwise.

With right needle, draw yarn back through the stitch.

Slide the stitch off the left needle. The new stitch is on the right needle.

Bind-Off

Binding Off (knit)

Knit first two stitches on left needle. Insert tip of left needle into first stitch worked on right needle and pull it over the second stitch and completely off the needle.

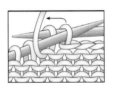

Knit the next stitch and repeat. When one stitch remains on right needle, cut yarn and draw tail through last stitch to fasten off.

Binding Off (purl)

Purl first two stitches on left needle. Insert tip of left needle into first stitch worked on right needle and pull it over the second stitch and completely off the needle.

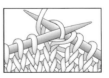

Purl the next stitch and repeat. When one stitch remains on right needle, cut yarn and draw tail through last stitch to fasten off.

Increase (inc)

Two Stitches in One Stitch

Knit in Front & Back of Stitch (kfb)

Knit the next stitch in the usual manner, but don't remove the stitch from the left needle. Place right needle behind left needle and knit again into the back of the same stitch. Slip original stitch off left needle.

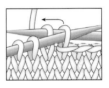

Purl in Front & Back of Stitch (pfb)

Purl the next stitch in the usual manner, but don't remove the stitch from the left needle. Place right needle behind left needle and purl again into the back of the same stitch. Slip original stitch off left needle.

Invisible Increase (M1)

There are several ways to make or increase one stitch.

Make 1 With Left Twist (M1L)

Insert left needle from front to back under the horizontal loop between the last stitch worked and next stitch on left needle.

With right needle, knit into the back of this loop.

To make this increase on the purl side, insert left needle in same manner and purl into the back of the loop.

Make 1 With Right Twist (M1R)

Insert left needle from back to front under the horizontal loop between the last stitch worked and next stitch on left needle.

With right needle, knit into the front of this loop.

To make this increase on the purl side, insert left needle in same manner and purl into the front of the loop.

Make 1 With Backward Loop Over the Right Needle

With your thumb, make a loop over the right needle.

Slip the loop from your thumb onto the needle and pull to tighten.

Make 1 in Top of Stitch Below

Insert tip of right needle into the stitch on left needle one row below.

Knit this stitch, then knit the stitch on the left needle.

Decrease (dec)

Knit 2 Together (k2tog)

Put tip of right needle through next two stitches on left needle as to knit. Knit these two stitches as one.

Purl 2 Together (p2tog)

Put tip of right needle through next two stitches on left needle as to purl. Purl these two stitches as one.

Slip, Slip, Knit (ssk)

Slip next two stitches, one at a time as to knit, from left needle to right needle.

Insert left needle in front of both stitches and knit them together.

Slip, Slip, Purl (ssp)

Slip next two stitches, one at a time as to knit, from left needle to right needle. Slip these stitches back onto left needle keeping them twisted. Purl these two stitches together through back loops.

I-Cord

Using 2 double-point needles, cast on (backward loop method) number of sts indicated. Knit, do not turn. Slip sts back to end of needle, knit sts. Repeat to desired length. Thread yarn through sts to end.

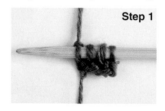 **Step 1**
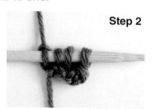 **Step 2**
 **Step 3**
 **Step 4**

Magic Loop Method

This method of working in the round uses one long circular needle, ideally one with a very flexible cable. It is very similar to working with two circular needles but many knitters prefer it to working with two needles because it eliminates the distracting loose ends of the second circular needle. Once you master this technique, it's a great solution when working on small-circumference projects.

Cast on or pick up the required number of stitches onto a 29-inch, or longer, circular needle. Slide the stitches to the cable portion of the needle. Pinch the cable in half as shown below, then pull to create a large loop. Arrange half the stitches on one needle tip, and half on the other.

Follow these 3 easy steps:

Step 1: The photo below shows how your stitches should look after you have distributed them on the two parts of the needle. The points of the needle and the "tail" from the cast on row are facing to the right and the cables are on your left.

Tip: After cast on row: refer to Working with Two Circular Needles to join the first and last stitch.

Step 2: The next step, as shown below illustrates how to begin working your first round: Hold the needle in your left hand, and pull out the needle that holds the "tail end"; the stitches that were on the needle

point are now resting on the cable. Begin working the stitches that are still on the opposite needle point as if you were working on straight needles.

Step 3: At the end of the row, simply turn the work around and reposition the stitches as shown. Once again, the needles are pointing to the right, and the cable loop is to the left.

Continue to work in this manner until desired length is reached.

The example below shows how the work will appear on the needle as the work gets longer.

Step 1

Step 2

Step 3

Step 4

Step 5

Pompoms

Cut two cardboard circles in size specified in pattern. Cut a hole in the center of each circle, about ½ inch in diameter. Thread a tapestry needle with a length of yarn doubled. Holding both circles together, insert needle through center hole, over the outside edge, and through center again (Figure 1) until entire circle is covered and center hole is filled (thread more length of yarn as needed).

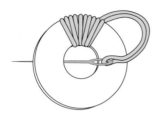

Figure 1

With sharp scissors, cut yarn between the two circles all around the circumference (Figure 2).

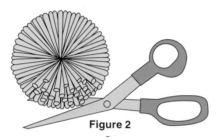

Figure 2

Using two 12-inch strands of yarn, slip yarn between circles and overlap yarn ends two or three times (Figure 3) to prevent knot from slipping, pull tightly and tie into a firm knot.

Remove cardboard and fluff out pompom by rolling it between your hands. Trim even with scissors; leave the tying ends for when attaching pompom to project.

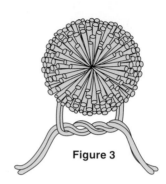

Figure 3

Resources

. . . .

Berroco Inc.
1 Tupperware Drive
Suite 4
North Smithfield, RI 02896-6815
(401) 769-1212
www.berroco.com

Cascade Yarns
1224 Andover Park E.
Tukwila, WA 98188
(206) 574.0440
www.cascadeyarns.com

Classic Elite Yarns
122 Western Ave.
Lowell, MA 01852
(800) 343-0308
www.classiceliteyarns.com

Dream in Color
www.dreamincoloryarn.com

Plymouth Yarn Co.
500 Lafayette St.
Bristol, PA 19007
(215) 788-0459
www.plymouthyarn.com

**Spinrite Inc.
(Caron)**
320 Livingstone Ave. South
Box 40
Listowel, ON
N4W 3H3 Canada
(800) 888 368 8401 (Patons)
www.caron.com

Universal Yarn Inc.
5991 Caldwell Business Park Drive
Harrisburg, NC 28075
(704) 789-YARN (9276)
www.universalyarn.com

Westminster Fibers
165 Ledge St.
Nashua, NH 03060
800.445.9276
www.westminsterfibers.com

Blumenthal Lansing Co.
30 Two Bridges Rd. Suite 110
Fairfield, NJ 07004
800-448-9749
www.blumenthallansing.com

Meet the Designer

. . . .

Knitting became a career for Carri Hammett when she opened her yarn shop, Coldwater Collaborative, in 2002. Being surrounded by gorgeous yarn and working as a retailer inspired her to begin designing for her customers. Carri was discovered by a publisher and started writing books in 2005. She has a passion for writing books that make knitting easy to understand and that inspire readers to learn new skills. She also loves to use her knowledge of quilting and crafting to create unexpected and fresh designs like knitted quilts and greeting cards. After selling her yarn shop in 2010, Carri now works full time as a knitting writer and designer. She has written five books (available on Amazon) and numerous articles for *Creative Knitting*. Visit her website for information about her books, patterns and kits at www.coldwateryarn.com. •

More Than a Dozen Hats & Beanies is published by Annie's, 306 East Parr Road, Berne, IN 46711. Printed in USA. Copyright © 2012, 2018 Annie's. All rights reserved. This publication may not be reproduced in part or in whole without written permission from the publisher.

RETAIL STORES: If you would like to carry this pattern book or any other Annie's publications, visit AnniesWSL.com.

Every effort has been made to ensure that the instructions in this pattern book are complete and accurate. We cannot, however, take responsibility for human error, typographical mistakes or variations in individual work. Please visit AnniesCustomerService.com to check for pattern updates.

ISBN: 978-1-59217-393-8
11 12 13

Photo Index

6

8

10

13

16

18

20

22

25

28

30

32

34

36

38